L. R. KANTZER
P9-CMS-995

We Lived With Dying

We Lived With Dying

Margaret Woods Johnson

WORD BOOKS
Waco, Texas

We Lived With Dying

Printed in the United States of America
Library of Congress catalog card number: 74-82656

Prologue

Summer, 1973

On a beautiful snowy day in January of '64, when my children were twenty-two, twenty, and fifteen, their father died of cancer after a seven-month fight. He was forty-nine and a Lutheran pastor in Washington, D.C. I was forty-seven. In the following two and a half years I slowly wrote these pages, addressing them to the three children—Mary Carol, a mother in her own home, Louise at college in Minnesota, and Stephen snoozing through school.

In January of 1973 my life in the little ecumenical Church of The Saviour here in Washington deepened into formal membership. Basic to our corporate life in Christ is the evoking, identifying and nurturing of the unique gifts in each of us. After I wrote my spiritual autobiography (one of the requirements at the point of entry into membership) and read it aloud to the church council, an old interior rumbling began to surface. If writing is my deepest gift, have I been called to sift out others more didactic and lucrative but less creative and less difficult, and focus on this one?

So these pages were recommitted, as my trumpet at morn, for I had written about two people under the same roof at the same point in time who looked at death with real interest and no fear, that I knew of. By sharing this unusual passage I hoped to increase a rightful enthusiasm for each man's next great venture.

As I looked back again between the lines of those seven months, it became apparent that I had written of other matters also, contingent on the light in the reader. I was surprised and moved by the perceptions of experience that were more than I knew at the time.

Illumination that is interpreted in fruitful, fresh ways is one characteristic of art, yet to my pilgrim-puritan-pioneer mind, art had been fluff. I had acknowledged sneakily for years that I loved being creative in homespun ways. Now I saw that by the deepest centering down possible for me to date, I had reflected in the manuscript gentle beauty unaware. The discovery gave me both wings and moans, for the depth of centering down that is required is barricaded daily by demonic objections to the necessary trading of my weak tools for God's surprising uses.

I was enabled to choose to appropriate this fragile gift of writing, to be accountable for it, and quietly to assay the external and internal spaces needed for its exercise. I mention it here for two reasons. Crucial universal issues rest on this exploration within everyone. And I wish I had known it years and years ago. I knew the world *seemed* right-side-up when you eat home-made bread, for instance. I didn't know it *comes* right side up when you meet the needs of your own mind in hard labor and deep joy, whatever your mode is. For you are thereby a little more acquainted with creativity, creation and the Creator, and a lot less impatient with previously frustrating sectors. You have put your talent into the marketplace for the exchange without price and thereby do not lose even that which you have been given.

To my three children

We have watched your dad go rapidly, heroically and knowingly through the bright doors of death after seven months with cancer.

During his illness I didn't understand why our Christian friends thought it extraordinary that neither of us was afraid of the next life, and that we spoke candidly of the evenly balanced chances he had for living or dying. I thought they shared our bright ideas of Eternity. How else is earth illumined and traversable?

Then several weeks after he died I realized that my happy thoughts of Heaven, begun and nurtured since childhood, and his more sober conviction of the shape of Eternity woven clearly beneath the clouded exteriors of struggle and hope, like the underside of our Oriental rugs where the patterns are so beautifully clear, had together formed a buoyant, expectant approach to the great unknown. And I now wanted to share this expectancy.

"Talk to me, Mama" was a byword in my girlhood home. All four of my mother's daughters loved to exchange their musings and moralizings with her, endlessly sharing the personal correlations of the inner and outer worlds of each of us. Our mother's cogitations startled, amused, annoyed and intrigued us, but we always knew what she was thinking about, beautifully daydreaming and wisdom-weaving in the middle of her ironing or cooking or dusting or mending.

The passion to think and talk and weave for meaning remains with me. In our twenty-five years together I probably plagued your dad with a need to talk and to have my ideas rearranged and polished up, when I should have done more of my own polishing. But my happiest memories are those of our searching conversations, whether impassioned or calm, lurid or lucid.

Once when perched beside him during his last hospital siege, I said,

"This is so hard. You're here now. But after awhile you won't be."

"I know," he answered. "But when you get there, we'll have some great conversations."

Now that I have no daily sparring partner, no daily wisdom-weaver for my mind, and you three have no father in the accustomed sense, I shall talk to you on paper, perhaps even more than we have in person, of my thoughts since your father's death. Our lack of fear was a unique gift, and in these vignettes I have tried to trace some of the reasons for it.

To any skeptical friends listening in I might say that I now love the Creator enough, so that if this life is all there is, then that is all right, too.

But I honestly don't think so.

I.

When Wayne came home late one winter evening early in 1963 and told me he had been having elusive, fingerlike pains in his side, he looked at me as though telling me he had deep forebodings. Months later when I asked him about it, he said he hadn't thought it was serious at all. But it was there in his eyes, as though his body knew and expressed what his mind hadn't yet taken in.

My over-active intuition told me it was serious. Later on the pains went to the other side and then vanished, and X-rays showed nothing. But the first of May he felt a lump in his abdomen. He mentioned it to no one and later gave three different reasons why he had put it out of his mind: he wanted to think it was part of his body; he wanted to think it would take care of itself; as a clergyman he wanted to complete a two-year period of religious instruction for young adolescents at the end of May.

I heard him give these three variations to three different people, the first two jokingly. The last was probably the real reason, for he cared greatly about that class, which included an unwed mother and a boy with leukemia who was to die before he did. As pastor of an integrated church in an inner city area of the District of Columbia, he had worked steadily to improve his methods of instruction to young adolescents. The Saturday morning study hours culminated in a service of confirmation on the festival day of Pentecost, that day when the Holy Spirit first empowered a group of new Christians in a way manifest to all.

So he put out of his mind the lump and the increasing weariness and lack of appetite that were creeping up on him. But after he died I found some notes for a talk he prepared that spring for a tiny midweek healing service. He had no medical knowledge then of cancer in him. I do not know how or whether he used the notes. They said in part

> Some insights—
>
> I am much more aware of the uncertainty of mortal life at a much deeper level, and of the certainty of God's care.
>
> I have a feeling that cancer is being

washed, driven out of me by a flood of prayer and love.

Live one day at a time.

Cancer is a threat to my being. Yet it is no such threat.

We can trust the truth: We are on solid ground.

Prayer opens up enormous resources.

Love becomes a visible reality.

Never minimize the priceless gift of natural sleep.

Aren't the last words touchingly human? His concern for himself cropped out in an unremembered spot, in his concern for healing others.

He was seldom aware of his own fatigue. He had worked sixty to eighty hours a week for twenty-five years, steadily, solidly. Jokingly that spring he said to his associate pastor,

"If I took a month's vacation right now, I wouldn't feel guilty."

It would seem that we all live on several levels at once. In lively playbacks of my memory some of his other levels are evident. When he preached about living life in an awareness of death, did he know at deeper levels in his own cells that something would be bringing him to a halt long before his retirement years? For his conscious mind had looked forward to that time when he would read all the books that he longed to get into.

In one of my playback memories the deep fatigue is very evident. In the last weekend in May we were both soloists in double concerts given by an inner-city school chorus of several hundred exuberant Negro youngsters. I can see him standing on the high old-fashioned stage of the school auditorium singing "Shenandoah" in his beautiful tenor voice. He was gray with weariness, but so enthralled with the children's singing of "Give me your tired, your poor, your huddled masses yearning to be free" and "This is *my* country, land of my *birth,*" that he went directly out and bought the songs. Those young ones almost shouted their proclamation in that huge barnlike room, and the sound was heart-rending in that impacted area of our capital city.

He had cared intensely about integration for many years. He couldn't say No to projects, people, problems. But he said Yes to some right ones, like singing with those youngsters, with one foot in heaven, as it were!

2.

In the first week of June that lump came into his ken again. At the same retreat camp above Harper's Ferry, where he had first felt it a month before, lying on his back on a firm camp cot, he slept not a wink and did all his worrying right then. He got up at 4:00 A.M., drove into Washington to the church and prepared material for the secretary. He was home at 9:00 to greet you, Louise, as you returned from your sophomore year at Gustavus Adolphus in Minnesota. Then to the doctor's where he was told he must check into the hospital that day, any time before midnight. More work and a meeting, and he went in at 11:30 P.M.

The following week he was operated on. I was writing letters in his room when the surgeon came in. I thought at first he was joking when he said,

"It's mighty serious. I give him a maximum of three months, although X-ray treatments might help some.

"Tell the family by all means, but don't tell your husband until he is past the possible nausea effects from the anaesthetic."

Wayne was brought down soon, but he remained unconscious a good while, long enough for me to examine my deep inclination to carry out an agreement we had made years before. We would tell each other the truth in just such matters as this. And I had had an experience of my own when Timmy, our fourth, was born and lived only those ten hours.

The obstetrician had immediately pierced my dense oblivion with a direct, loud,

"Mrs. Woods, Mrs. Woods. You're all right, but I'm not so sure about the baby."

When I woke up several hours later, I could cope with the not-new information that they didn't expect the baby to live. I was profoundly grateful that the truth had been given me directly and immediately.

So when your dad opened his eyes as from a distance and said, "Is it cancer?" I leaned on the bars of the bed and waited to see if he was conscious enough to ask again. The eyes were near and clear as he asked five seconds later,

"Is it?"

"Yes."

"Okay," he breathed, and slid back to sleep.

That evening when we were all around his bed he said weakly,

"Isn't it great that we don't have to fence around with the truth?"

3.

After the operation floods of cards came, and in response to them all, Wayne wrote from the hospital—

> One week and a day have passed since the momentous news (I was going to say shattering, but it hasn't been that) was given us that I have cancer. We had decided to face the truth openly. So here it was in all its nakedness. What did it mean? What would it mean?
>
> We all have a horrible image of cancer. We have seen and heard enough to convince us that it is just about the worst thing that could happen to us or anyone. The mind runs like a scared rabbit this way and that, into each frightening possibility until at last,

exhausted, it becomes quiet and still before the great wonder and mystery of God.

As a family we have found that life moves on and that our crooked image of cancer begins at once to change. So far, this close dark Brother is not as ugly as we thought, and in our house he hasn't proved to be such a terrible guest.

On the other hand there has been a veritable tidal wave of love and prayer coming from far and near. Prayer vigils, prayer groups, prayer poems. Each child in the Church school last Sunday wrote a prayer or sent some token of love. Many pastors have stopped in, each with his own habitual bedside ministry. There has been a steady stream of visitors and phone calls until some limits were needed.

Flowers, common and rare, mute spokesmen for the Spirit, have come in such numbers that one day in spritely mood I peddled them up and down the corridor to those who had none at all.

Cards from friends, a few with side-splitting humor or a series of riddles, the great bulk full of devout and poetic get-well sentiment, all designed to cheer and bless, plus letters from loved ones.

What an ocean of love and intercessory prayer we have suddenly found ourselves floating on! One can literally feel oneself being bathed in this mighty sea. At times I have been sure the cancer is being washed away.

Some things we have learned. We have become more vividly aware of the uncertainties of life and at the same time we have become more sure of God. We have started to live one day at a time, the usual long view ahead has been telescoped into a more grateful kind of day-to-day living. We have found what we long took for granted, that we can trust the truth. However hard or rocky, it is solid beneath the feet and dependable. We have been awakened to the tremendous resources of the Spirit, channeled to us through the Church. In all of this we have seen love become a visible reality before our eyes.

On the evening of the second day of X-ray treatments, the worst so far in the recovery period, I was panicking. All day I had been groggy, only half awake. My abdomen seemed to me to be slightly enlarging, crowding what little food I ate for supper. Into the center of my restlessness and fear suddenly Christ came. It dawned on me that He was in this with me. He would face with me whatever this night held. He told me this in secret. Quickly I calmed down and I heard God saying in a grand full slow voice, "I am healing you. I AM HEALING YOU." My fears passed and that night was my best night of rest.

One good friend and leader in the

congregation, a Negro principal of a white school, wrote me, "I have always been a firm believer in the power of prayer, and was perfectly honest with God as I prayed—even as Noah in *Green Pastures.* I wanted Him to know that I knew I was praying for a very big favor that was contrary to medical beliefs."

I shall never forget two weeks ago, on my first day here, when my doctor asked me to visit a Lutheran patient who was not expected to live through that day. His heart was the size of a cantaloupe and all the signs were negative. I saw him three times the first day and three times the second, and tried to get him in touch with God. I talked with his wife and had short sessions with him each day until my operation. The power of God to heal had reversed the negatives into positives. He is out of the oxygen tent, getting up and gaining strength each day, to the amazement of those in charge. My doctor, a devout Christian, smiles knowingly to me as he reports his progress. I can only wonder and rejoice in the love and power of God.

Wrap it all up—the man across the hall calling insistently "Somebody"; the horrible moment when the nose hose intended for my stomach went down my windpipe; the sickness following the multiple enemas prior to barium X-ray pictures; the long days and nights; the friendly banter of the nurses; the X-ray

treatments, nine minutes daily under the
gurgling, humming, high-pitched metallic
slow tremolo of the great green machine—
wrap it all up and it's the deepest two weeks
of our lives.

Dear
Paster
Woods

I hope
you will
be beder
soon. God
well. bles you and
ceep you.

I no how you
feel. I hope
you will feel

Ricky Hoffman

4.

The men at the X-ray machine said they had seen worse lymph system cases than your father's cleared up with treatments. Medically, spiritually, humanly, no one knows whether this case or that will make it. A few weeks earlier our doctor had told a woman that her husband was not going to pull out of a severe liver disease, and yet the man was at home, well.

So our days were balanced perfectly on a "will we?" or "won't we?" that actually seemed to give us vitality rather than otherwise. Only once, in the middle of those months, did I have a long crying spell.

"Go right ahead and cry, kid," Wayne said. "It's good that you can."

All the gradual debilitation, which was remarkably little up to the seventieth treatment, could be laid to the treatments themselves. I'm fairly sure our friends jumped to their own conclusions immediately, while we understandably couldn't. I had told a friend just before the operation, without really knowing that I thought it,

"He had pains here and here, and now a lump here. I think he's full of cancer and not going to last long."

Yet a whole other half of my mind held all the solid assumption that he really might come through.

The woeful looks of other people were harder to cope with than the inner situation itself. Although I hadn't the dimmest notion of what it would be like to be on my own after twenty-five years of marriage, I know that your dad and I never granted any finality to death. When you know and care about a person, the knowing and the caring continue, with tremendously greater possibilities for knowing and caring and communicating at the later date we call Eternity.

We certainly knew each other in both severe and jovial ways. After he came home from the hospital and his whole tenuous relation to the land of the living changed, the enforced relaxation brought on some reconstruction pains. As he slowly lowered himself into a chaise in the lazy June sunshine, he said with almost groaning humility,

"You'll have to help me with this. I'm used to going to work."

I stood still.

He had worked very hard "for God" without often tasting His sweetness, perhaps because theological tasks get traded too easily for the quiet centering down that is their source.

By contrast, I had developed a great need to know the Eternal in direct, personal terms, and the reality of Jesus had become a steadily worked-at gift. At heart I have been a Quaker, searching the silences for nourishment. Wayne may have sensed that he now had to climb across from the familiar public ecclesiastical arena into the internal domain of his private drama. ("Climb across" is the literal meaning of *transcend.*)

He began to labor with his feelings, to find the Kingdom within, day after day. After years of commitment to the church "out there" he realized he had neglected its great potentials at home. Although as you said later, Stephen, "But when you really needed him, he was there." And Steve had been able to count on two overnight hikes each year with him on the Appalachian Trail.

Now, instead of rarely seeing him, we had him with us all the time. Instead of being shut off from us in preoccupations with church life and problems, he became open, warm and grateful. I had rarely been able to claim his presence and friendship as against the claims we both responded to from parishioners.

Now he was given to us.

Even more, he had reached out for help with his pains, which set us in true community. We could no longer be busily righteous "out there." It was the beginning of the greatest change I have been privileged to see.

Did our guests think we were gallantly facing doom? We didn't think so.

Many years before, from Aldous Huxley's *Time Must Have a Stop,* I had picked up a sense that each man's path to Eternity can be uniquely luminous. Bruno lies dying with cancer of the throat, conveying in his eyes and in the notes he jots to Sebastian, the tender joy of what he saw of the Here and the There. He walked with anticipation and awe into his next dimension.

I honestly carried a feeling that Wayne was on a privileged path. We lived with life and death as one interwoven entity. What looked like doom on the home front was inwardly a gift of seven months together. After twenty-five years of zeal and "never being home," we had twenty-eight weeks of "gift living," totally unexpected and gratefully received.

We sat in the sun in chaises on the upper terrace of our little backyard, looking into the skies through the huge oaks and maples of this quiet old community adjacent to Washington. He drove himself to the Adventist hospital almost daily for treatments. We went to movies. Isn't it odd that we felt free to do that only because we could do so little else? We sipped root beer floats with innumerable guests. He was lionized and he knew it. What if he had been eighty and alone and battling with cancer?

"Nobody would pay any attention to me," he said quite accurately.

5.

When Mary Carol recently came across some famous lines by Thoreau, she had a startling new appreciation of her husband.

"You know," said she, "when David and I disagree, it may be that he is hearing a different drummer than I am!"

As I trace the reasons why the prospect of loss of life did not panic your father, I think of the different drummers through the years that he listened to. They were not the conventional ones of success, attainments, prestige.

At our first parish in 1938, Wayne welcomed with great relish the lowest church on the Pittsburgh Synod's totem pole. In the slum section of Soho, the little congregation that worshiped in a large ugly edifice couldn't manage mortgage, repairs, or a living wage to the pastor, although they were furred, bejewelled citizens who had fled to the suburbs in disdain of poorer latecomers. They were hold-the-line nay-sayers, bemoaning the rough neighborhood and tolerating with tongue in cheek both Wayne and Henry, the young Sunday school superintendent. Those two visited all the neighborhood Sunday school pupils and their families with zest, cameraderie and vision.

Great readers both, they quoted to each other such lines as William Blake's

To see a world in a grain of sand,
And heaven in a wild flower;
Hold infinity in the palm of your hand,
And eternity in an hour.

They saw eternity in the children's faces, woe and courage in the parents', and tragedy in the congregation and the church-at-large. The sturdy pair knew how Christ wept over the least of these, our brethren, and over those who neither went in nor let anybody else go in to the heavens of this hour.

When we chose the rickety-rackety slums to live in, as well as work in, we were hearing a drummer out of Japan. Kagawa's passionate, selfless, capable devotion to his country's poor had made a great impression on us during our college years. When Wayne and Henry tramped up and down the Soho slums, they were part of a vulnerable band around the world whose hearts are fortunately expendable. They could ache and break over the multiply deprived who are usually such a threat to the rest of us.

When we chose voluntary poverty as a way of living, we were part of a small band around the world who value simplicity and perhaps shore up necessity, but we also saw the point to buying what we *really* needed. What we thought we needed changed during the years. I grant you that voluntary poverty is much easier than involuntary, but we valued the discipline of spending our money in relation to larger issues and needs. Few people understood any explanation of *that* drum, rolled up mixture that it is of unselfishness, a Spartan life, and unhealthy self-denial. We learned early how to be abased, and later how to abound, in a manner of speaking. It has to remain a reversible procedure though, especially in the approach to death. "You can't take it with you" was not a righteous byword in our house but a reminder of what we *can* take with us, stripped down to a bare capacity for courage, individuality and compassion.

Before the Second World War we had heard another rare drum—the need for reconciliation and nonviolent aggression, the willingness to say, "I can lose now so we can all win later." Gandhi's impact on India and Britain, his vision, discipline and soul force, went to the marrow of our bones. My logic said, "Somebody's got to eat humble pie." And Wayne's logic added, "And you've got to develop guts to do it." We also pondered the thought that "the only causes worth fighting for are the lost causes." Everybody else takes up for the popular ones.

In the early fifties in a painful siege in our second parish when a Negro friend asked to join the church and the council turned him down, seven to five, Wayne saw it as a little skirmish in a long, long battle for real brotherhood in the Christian church. He could lose the skirmish with more equanimity than I could, for he knew that it had taken the Quakers a hundred years to get rid of their slaves, and that Lincoln had held on firmly to the opposing sides that were equally convinced of their own positions.

In the civil rights march on Washington in August 1963, here in our third parish, Wayne participated in a borrowed wheelchair, sharing in the gala spirit of a hundred thousand valiant souls from all over the country. He felt his effort small compared to the expenditures of energy needed to effect each gain in a tremendous fight for justice. I think your father always saw his own humiliation, endurance, hope and pain in the larger context of humanity's hope, pain and endurance. He heard a vaster drumbeat, and it sustained him mightily in the months of his personal struggle.

6.

We had had some experience of deliberately trusting the grace of God and consciously facing the unknown and the uncomfortable a good while before we were in the intense seven months of "not-knowing" in 1963.

Twice in the early years we had taken careful soundings and charted an unsafe course. After eight years with the first little congregation in the slums, we went to our second parish in another section of Pittsburgh. We had wanted a taste of greenery and so moved to those two beautiful acres five miles out the road from the church itself.

As the skirmish over integration approached (which affected me as a major battle), we felt too safe and too distant. After five years with the vegetables and flowers and chickens, I prayed to do as Abraham had done—to go where we were told to go. It was my first experience of great light and a clear answer. Next day we found the house with the kitchen big enough to ski in and the sidewalks you wanted. For the next five years we lived there two blocks from the church.

Your dearest friends were black; our powers of appreciation were increased. But the majority of the congregation couldn't assimilate the conditions of change in their immediate neighborhood. Perhaps they had more resistance than some, for they had had only one other pastor during their whole forty-six-year life—your Grandpa Woods. The mixed feelings they had for his less orthodox son may have precluded the humility necessary to listen to Wayne's farthest vision. They were not able to ask the Lord to loosen their restraints and accept one black member. A salty old woman told me, "Anybody else could'a made us do it."

Our first congregation had eschewed its community also, in an earlier decadence, and we had struggled in its near atrophy. Slow death is painful to watch. We couldn't spark enough life in this second one to delay or reverse the process.

At that moment of discouragement, an article appeared in the *Reader's Digest* about a little ecumenical congregation in Washington, D.C. My Baptist background had helped conflict us right into an openness for a nondenominational approach, where integrity of membership in the Body of Christ seemed central. We wanted to be among folks who were changing the wineskins, instead of saying "it can't be done," and we knew we needed some new wine ourselves.

We decided to see what gave them their reputed zip. In '56, when you were fifteen, thirteen, and eight, we took soundings again, pulled up stakes and headed for D.C. I noticed that none of you doubted our invigorating joint decision. We put into the venture the equity in the house with the big kitchen and didn't know what else we would have to live on during the self-propelled sabbatical.

Two lines sustained me.

"For my God shall supply all your needs according to his riches in glory." It was one of our table graces when I was a girl. "There will be money for what we *really* need," I pronounced to myself axiomatically.

And every once in a while I sang at the kitchen sink Samuel Wesley's

> For it is Thou, Lord, Thou Lord only,
> Who makest me dwell in safety.

That helped. It has a funny, croaky tune but it did the trick.

After ten months in one precarious section of the business world, your dad joyfully became associate pastor of the National Augustana Lutheran Church, already committed to its inner-city community and wrestling with integration. High seas, indeed! When we first sat together in their beautiful miniature cathedral, Bach's great song, "Sheep May Safely Graze," was sung. I could hardly believe my ears and thought with astonishment, How marvelously apropos!

We had only one definition of security. "If you put what you've got into life, life will take care of you."

We had twice set sail on unknown seas, relying on the winds of God—very unsafe in worldly terms. There were times of travail. The complexities of team leadership of a congregation committed to community involvement pulled me in one direction. At the same moment came my first professional experience with the visually impaired students in the public schools to the east of D.C. I floundered somewhere between. Wayne loved being in harness with an equally hard-working brother whose zaniness and poetics matched his own. When the senior pastor and his wife went off to a Protestant congregation in Saudi Arabia, Wayne continued to seek at Augustana a viable concept of "church." Only after ten months did he get an associate.

Our own relationship pulled mighty thin. In desperation, some time in the two years before he died, I learned to say (always on his day off so none of you heard),

"Let's have a *good* fight. Not one with acrimony."

Would you believe such polite language?

It was a tardy beginning of a healthy confrontation of dread territories in ourselves and each other. The seas didn't get smoother. We got more rugged. And we saw there were great rewards in sailing squarely into the unknown.

7.

When Wayne had to be out of church life all of June and July and could not attend any and every church meeting, he had the delicious experience of knowing he was not indispensable. I think something had been jarred loose in him earlier in the spring!

Some weeks before he was operated on, at one of those ministers' conferences, he heard a true story from a fellow-pastor, and he came home chortling over it.

In the annual to-do of getting pledges for next year's budget, the fellow-pastor had a campaign chairman who kept promising airily that the committee would be made up shortly, the planning meetings would be scheduled immediately, everything was rolling, don't worry, I'm taking care of it. This went on for several weeks, but it was quite evident that nothing was happening.

"Finally," said the pastor, "I made an act of faith. I said, 'The hell with it!' "

In the role of inspiring thrifty people to open their purses in ways they can later be proud of, I think it is agony for the pastor to have his own pride masked as responsible leadership, when perhaps he is just playing papa to people's prolonged adolescence. And it seems to be agony to have his identity tied in with the success or failure of a group of people who both demand and reject parental shepherding—and pay his salary besides!

Wayne took seriously the nature, function and goals of the Church, especially of the inner-city churches which struggle with all the problems of the impacted areas. Our church had not fled to suburbia but had dug in, built an educational unit, and now hoped to cope with complex challenges. This kind of financial burden seems more valid than some fancier ones I can think of. Wayne really wanted to see the indebtedness lifted.

But here was his fellow-minister saying as an act of faith re the financial sweat,

"The hell with it!"

As I write it, I laugh again. What could be more gorgeously free—free to fail, free to lose, free to goof, free from the strangling necessity to succeed, free from one small ego-clutch and pride-hold! An innate right to feel *un*beholden for everything in a congregation asserted itself vigorously. With his great laugh, a burden rolled off Wayne's shoulders. He seemed delivered from needing to succeed financially, professionally, physically. Nothing is that important—neither budgets nor projects nor members nor programs—save the unique life of a given soul.

As his body was losing health, his spirit was gaining life.

8.

To those who constantly sent expressions of love he responded with this second letter, July 28th.

Dear Friends,

It is six blessed weeks back to that terrible and exciting day when I opened my eyes after the operation and asked Margaret point-blank, "Is it cancer?" and she answered, "Yes."

The surgeon had told her, "He has three months at the maximum." He had found extensive evidence of cancer located in the lymphatic system of the mesentery, a structural tissue holding the small intestines in place. Other areas were involved near the spine and aorta. It was inoperable.

Three days later a report on the sample sent

to the lab showed a fast-growing variety of cancer cell, which is highly susceptible to damage by exposure to X-ray radiation. At this news the surgeon said he was more optimistic.

Six days after the operation I received the first of a projected daily series of 48 X-rays—nine minutes, Monday through Friday, under a huge machine which sounds like a jet engine about ready for the take-off.

Today I will get the 26th treatment. The usual side effects—nausea, diarrhea, lack of energy—have been mild or nonexistent in my case. I have lost some 20 pounds of weight, have regained about five.

We live from day to day, trusting in the loving help of God. I have been lolling in the sun, taking longer and longer walks. Each day I feel stronger.

Apparently the X-rays have taken hold. Such minor pains as have come, have disappeared. *We believe I am on the way toward a full recovery.*

Margaret and the children have given me the most loving care and consideration. We've been able to attend church together. It's a rare treat for us to be sitting in the same pew. We have also taken some short trips in the car and have been to some movies.

I want to express to you an intense gratitude. I have felt myself lifted and carried on an ocean of love and prayer. Your kindness and affection and faith and prayers, I can never forget.

Many wonderful blessings have drenched us in this experience: A new revealing of God's healing power and love; a new realization of the Church as a loving, praying, ministering, healing community; a sense of participation in the human drama at deeper levels; insights into what others have to undergo in a hospital experience; a sense of judgment and deliverance; the comfort of facing and trusting the truth; new dimensions of understanding and comfort in the Scriptures; a new sense of the healing, strengthening presence of Christ; the bliss of being able to be at home.

So, we rejoice in these blessings and send with this letter our thankfulness to you and our love.

Wayne R. Woods and Family

On August 14th he revised the mimeographed letter to say, "Such minor pains as have come have mostly disappeared."

In September he revised it further.

A persistent ache in the right shoulder in early August proved to be cancer of the bone. Treatments on my abdomen were discontinued after the 40th one and begun on my shoulder—three a week with a somewhat heavier dosage of the powerful rays. That series of ten was completed.

Respiratory difficulties have developed and we discovered a small surface lump above the left lung. So, I have begun another set of daily X-ray treatments on the chest area. The doctors claim that worse areas than mine have been brought under control and the cancer arrested.

The type of cancer I have is quelled by the X-rays but it breaks out easily in other places. So we continue to pray and to hope that recovery will eventually come. I have never been so grateful for life.

There are times when we are discouraged. The thought that I may be in my last days on earth is both sobering and exciting. The prospect of soon entering upon the Life-to-Come holds some supreme and shining adventures. We are learning to entrust our lives to God and to live one day at a time.

I am daily engaged in some work at the Church. For the time being I will be preaching regularly on Sundays, having shifted more of the administrative responsibilities to Pastor Lundeen.

We continue to consider ourselves greatly blessed and continue to bask in the love of God, whom Paul Tillich calls "the Ground of our Being." How thrilling it is to realize that Reality—ultimate Reality—is the love we see embodied in Jesus Christ, and that He is alive and with us today.

Thanks again for your prayers, your concern, your love.

Wayne

9.

I wasn't able to pray for healing for your dad, perhaps because of my experience in praying for Louise. When she was eight years old we realized that she had eyes that would never see all that we see. At thirteen we discovered that those eyes would probably see less and less as time went on. I took a running leap into books on spiritual healing. I prayed up a storm in fancy terms and plain ones. Praise be, it was the beginning of my own spiritual pilgrimage.

One of the fanciest terms of those years was "prayer power," and there were even subtle status symbols to show that you had some. We had none. Louise's eyes have not been restored. But Wayne and I changed and you all changed and Louise became our troubadour, as well as everyone else's. She had always been a gift. Now she became our growing edge.

And what growth! We read to her one to four hours a day, five and six days a week, until exhaustion took over and I for one moaned,

"You have got to learn Braille."

It was because of my experience with her that I worked with partially seeing students in the public schools, telling them and their teachers and their parents that they *perceive plenty* with all their senses, and that they are handicapped only if they consider themselves unable to tackle new things.

We shunned pity and knew that in her constellation of life factors she had much more going for her than against her. We saw her with her back to many an educational and social wall, learning to pray and discovering over and over again that there were marvelous solutions to agonizing impasses. We saw her develop enormous humor, poise, sensitivity and initiative.

We weren't her helpers. She was ours.

As imperious pray-ers we felt sure there must be some hallowed wavelength that would bring perfect cell structure to those eyes. And there probably is. But as fumbling kneelers we laid an altar to perfect eyesight and saw the fire descend instead into our frail family, warming and humanizing our pedestrian hearts. We had wanted one showy miracle and got five quiet ones.

So by the time your dad had cancer, I didn't have the temerity to ask for healing. For a long time Louise's eyesight had seemed like a life-and-death issue. And at times it still does. I die several small grief-deaths each year over what she ought to be able to see—people's loving eyes, and the print she would devour so eagerly if she could. But the silver lining of grief is gift, and you perceive people's qualities without seeing the glints. And all over the world folks "read" with fingertips or ears as broadly as they want to.

So grief-death has become gift-life over and over again. And perhaps I knew this when Wayne was ill. I had passionately wanted Louise to see, more than anything else in the world. I didn't get my own way, didn't get physical healing. So there was no success pattern of whispering a soul-need in God's tender ear and knowing I would receive it, per Jesus' instructions. Grief had turned into a gift too often for me to insist that one answer only could constitute life. There are many kinds of life and many varieties of death, and we don't often know which is which ahead of time!

As the seven months of illness went on, we received compassion, endurance, gratitude and joy. In his munificent provision the Eternal bestowed his choicest items—very real life and very real death woven in a very close pattern.

10.

I'd like to trace some of the reasons why I found myself unafraid of death.

When I was a young child, my mother was hard put to answer some of my intense questions, such as "How do I know I'm not adopted? Why do I turn in at this house instead of at some other house?"

Only when she was carrying her youngest and I her eldest was five, did I get an answer that satisfied me. As I put my hand on her stomach and perceived that babies grew in a "warm nest below the heart," only then was I content with believing that I had arrived that way too, and belonged at that house.

When it came to questions about death, she wasn't daunted at all, bless her. She said, in the first place, it happens to everyone. This gave me a great sense of sharing one definite experience with everybody, and that it therefore couldn't be too bad, since it was a common process. She also came up with this brilliant analogy: When a baby is in the womb, it is warm, content, cared for. But to come out into a cold world where it has to start breathing on its own! This must be a scary proposition to an infant, said Mama. Feeling snugly on this side of having learned to breathe alone, I saw how ridiculous it might be to die and look back and wonder what I had been so scared of before.

This all amounted to great intuitive logic to me. But emotionally another ingredient was put into my cheerful assumption that death was an acceptable next step. My father taught me some Bible passages when I was eleven and sick-a-bed for several months. He had lost a first wife and infant son in childbirth many years before, and now I glimpse what stirred him so deeply as he stood at the foot of the bed reciting,

"In my Father's house are many mansions. . . ."

To my young mind then this amounted to deepest certitude. Now my adult mind wonders if he too was looking forward to some great unfinished conversations, yearning for the growth of mind and soul that our several greatest relationships can bring to us, the mansions of insight and joy and wisdom-weaving that we call the communion of the saints.

I'm treading where I'm only guessing, as to my

dad. For myself, I have been happily expectant for a long, long time of the days when I'll be able to ask some questions of St. Paul and Luther, and hang around and listen while they talk together. Or maybe they won't be talking at all. Maybe I will come upon them extending humble ministrations to folk both here and there who wouldn't understand their big words and concepts at all.

Believing that I would some day look back and see life from a different perspective with fully open eyes, I have in these latter years found myself imagining what that ultimate perspective is, right now. This may be a reversed way of struggling to grow here and now, but it is a beginning. I had always known there would be joy and beauty in heaven, so I wanted to begin to be able to see it here and now.

Long before your dad died I thought about the next life, perhaps with an exuberant over-confidence and an undertow of hope that things would be easier there than here. But my picture of Heaven had several sober sides, too.

What if we grow so little here on earth that when we die we won't be in any shape to know we're *in* Heaven? This has very delicate applications to our earth-life. Maybe most of us can't see the heavenly aspects of each present day, and are missing much more than we dream of.

The I-want-to-win part of me comes right alive at the thought of being in some shape to recognize Heaven when I get there. If I am presented over There with several acquaintances who are unattractive conundrums right now, with whom I am to share a corner of Heaven's comely gardens, I had better start now to see their gemmy qualities and learn to love them. This has prodded me into more embarrassing prayers and humiliations than I will recount.

Somewhere along the line I picked up the school of thought that anticipates "in the twinkling of an eye . . . we shall all be changed," presumably into 100 percent love, compassion and praise. This may well be true, especially in a desire to be 100 percent giving and adoring. But my slightly logical mind says that we will want to be helping all creation praise Him, so we will ache to bring joy into all creatures in both dimensions, and will not be sitting up there in a still-life adoration, but will take on spiritual chores, there and here.

My confidence in the Creator's love may be overlooking something somewhere, but I can accept neither eternal damnation nor eternal nothingness. If we have to see all the ramifications of all our wrongs, and ache over all the minutiae, and desire infinitely to do it all over again, this may well be hell, and I have tasted it.

But I reason thus: God is love, little though we partake of Him. Love, God himself, "keeps no statistics of evil," as J. B. Phillips translates it. In our own moments of purest love in our gift relationships do we have any desire for punishment for past sins? I ask you, how then can the Creator do that?

I think men thought up judgment in order to wreak their own wrath in holy terms. Only God could think up mercy, and He did. When humans want other humans to change, they point the finger and say, "You'll be sorry" in thunderous, dogmatic terms.

When God wanted humans to change and return His love, He didn't shake the finger or the earth or the heavens. He didn't even give to the nature of love the capacity to demand love in return. Love is only happy to love—boundless, running over, ever-joyful, ever-merciful, ever-provident, ever-restoring.

If it takes a season of hellish awareness to restore us to loving Him back, then we can be grateful for the Refiner's fire. But everlasting love, too gracious and bashful to declare and demand, is everlasting love. And it was this insight that first brought me to profound awe and gratitude and attempted obedience to our Lord God Creator.

Is it not logical that any native capacity we have to trust the Source of our life and grow in that Source is only constricted and choked by threatened judgment and threatened punishment? Amazed gratitude, on the other hand, releases us and starts the joy and creativity rolling back to Him.

Even if the next life holds painful awareness and painful growth, will it not all the more hold joyful awareness and joyful growth?

II.

When I majored in English in college I learned a little about John Henry Cardinal Newman, a British scholar, preacher and priest. As an Anglican preacher he changed his mind and became a Catholic priest. When I learned that, I said "Hooray!" He had thought through his own concepts and had taken steps to be "all of a piece," and that calls for some flag-waving.

Then I discovered that he had written some marvelous lines in an old-fashioned hymn that a pious aunt of mine used to sing very somberly. When I developed enough temerity to sing it vigorously and in strict time, she raised a musical eyebrow and sighed a religious sigh.

In the fall of 1938 Wayne was interim pastor for two months in the English-speaking church in Berlin. When the organist asked me to sing a modest solo, we both had a gleeful zest at restoring "Lead, Kindly Light" to its intended vigor and disciplined swing. You will need to sing and play it yourselves to hear what I mean.

Anyway, here was my literary, churchly friend, John Henry, saying,

> "I do not ask to see
> The distant scene—one step enough for me."

Mr. Dykes, who set it to music, knew what he was doing when he swung the tune up to a high gorgeous emphasis on the very thing John Henry was saying he would survive without knowing—the distant scene!

I doubt that either the American ambassador or the other dignitaries in the service that Sunday heard one single word from the greenhorns in pulpit and choir loft. I myself don't remember clicking on those very lines that day. The ones that did reach me then were the last ones,

> And with the morn those angel faces smile
> Which I have loved long since, and lost awhile.

As I stood in the choir loft near the organist I remember feeling John Henry's ache for the dear faces he would see again. During my singing I felt a pure compassion for the scholarly poet. He was without those loved countenances *for a while.*

As a twenty-one-year-old I didn't know what

confidence the sure high gorgeous lines were weaving in me, any more than the ambassador, perhaps, had consciously gained courage for the "moors, crags and fens" of politics and poem.

I doubt that Wayne or I consciously remembered *any* hymns that fall when we sat opposite each other at the high kitchen bar at mealtimes, wordless, patient, while he tried to eat. We had no conscious notion of where our courage came from. In fact we didn't think we had any. But through the years there had been sung into our sinews the clearest insights of many buoyed-up, whittled-down human beings, and we therefore had more tensile strength than we knew.

His head was propped on his hand, meal after meal, week after week. There was no bitterness, no bravado, no blame in his face. The gentle appreciative words that came across that high table are still with me. Literally, neither of us had to see the distant scene, and one step, one bite, was enough.

As I sense again the quality of those hours, I keep thinking that we sat there well aware of a larger context. We quivered but did not quail. And part of the reason lay in the transparency of our countenances to each other. I'm wrestling with a huge thought here, and I'm going all around Barlow's Knoll to find a way to say it.

When countenances have ever been transparent to each other, when the greater Light of our being has ever shown through our faces in our knowing and living and caring, then there is no question at all of seeing and knowing those same countenances in Eternity.

I am positive that as we sat there in a humble "not knowing" of the distant scene, we had no doubt that we would perceive, behold, be transparent to each other at a later date.

I think this is one large reason why we weren't in the least afraid of death, *for*—

The countenances we have loved, do love, and will love, we will love forever, and be nourished by forever.

Isn't that great?

Maybe I shouldn't leave you with such a spritely theology, but it's some of the profoundest of my life.

We do live forever, all of us, and in recognizable semblance to each other. We will perceive in each other at least as much as we perceive now, and we will grow in that perception, mutual nourishment and joy, from more to more.

I think God was saying something loud and clear to us, to relieve our minds of dark forebodings, when Jesus was seen after his death in a semblance of great radiance.

All matter is some form of light, varying kinds of energy, and we change over into another form!

I used to think that when I got to Heaven I would know a person only in proportion to as much as I had perceived right here of his compassion, illumined praise, and humility. I wouldn't see his familiar physical aspects but only his real character. This would imply that perhaps only the wavelengths of joy, glory and love are carried over from here to There.

That's a thumping good theory but a tough one. For there are moments when, if we died right then, we would be in no shape to recognize the Lord Himself, all joy in us being swallowed by despair. Much less would we be able to perceive any dimmer lights in a loved one from this earlier life.

Now I have changed my mind and I think that I'll perceive on some great new wavelength your dad's countenance, eyebrows, chin, kind glance and all. I don't think this is stuffy or wishful thinking. In fact it's just the opposite. We're all going to see each other recognizably in our next life, so the countenances we don't welcome here and now, we had better do something about, as we're all going to live together forever.

We are all *in*, like it or not.

So what are we afraid of about death? Actually we have the Creator all mixed up with punishment, which is a backhanded way of dealing out justice to ourselves!

The Creator is far busier with joy and mercy and grace, and He has entertained a modest hope that we will want to enjoy Him and serve Him forever.

This positively shames us and releases us. Here we deserve endless sizzling, and He isn't interested in thermal heat rays! We are attuned to remorse and regret, and He says He's not dealing them out this Aeon.

Does He mean that we're supposed to cheer up and get on with the joy?

Yes, He does.

And not only that.

He's supplying it.

I think we know this in a dim corner of our brains, almost atrophied. We're not totally surprised by this joy because it is indigenous to us. We've tasted it, revelled in it, yearned for more, clutched it.

And gradually we learn its Source and seek Him instead of His gift, unclutching.

And the gift comes, too.

12.

While trying to write this I found myself telling the Lord I didn't want to be a Christian for a couple of weeks. I have forgotten what brought it on. I was probably tired of trying to live up to some "good" image of myself.

Then I had to laugh, for *telling* Him is part of the hard core joy of *being* a Christian.

The first spring we were at the Church of The Saviour, I was working on the word *redemption* for a class in the School of Christian Living. We each had to give a talk on the subject, but *only* out of our experience. On Easter afternoon, after half a lifetime of trying to keep a dutifully pious attitude toward the profundities of the church year, I casually, top-of-my-head-like, said to Jesus,

"I don't understand Easter at all."

What an answer I got, in words and concepts I could understand, while sorting clothes the next morning at the laundry table. My honest statement brought clear illumination.

Years ago I told your dad in granitelike fury that I couldn't abide one of you three. Praise heaven, he didn't advise me "not to feel that way." He looked at me in solid, alive silence and took it in without judgment. I well remember the quality of his participation in my terrible, unmotherly statement. That rock-bottom emotional honesty was the turning point in a relationship that now means great joy to me.

I'm drawing a small analogy here. It's fairly natural for one part of our nature to love, adore and respond to the Creator and His creation. There is another part of us that couldn't care less, that disbelieves our own best moments, and that can hardly bring to mind anything but the residual garbage and clutter inside us.

Somewhere along the line we have picked up the idea that only our best flowers, constructions, and perfumes are fair incense to the Lord. So we keep the well-embroidered side of the screen toward Him, and the side with the knots and tangles toward ourselves, imagining that He isn't on this side, too.

Isn't that pathetic? He's the Lord of the universe. He knows everything. He cares minutely about us at depth and has told us we stand free in His love and provision. And we imagine that our doubts and furies and squalors could knock Him over. Tsk! They are knocking us over, like unleashed cannonballs rolling on the decks of a ship in stormy seas.

Well, the Lord wants to tie up the cannonballs Himself, seeing that it's beyond us to do so, or else pitch them out with Paul Bunyan strength. But He pays us the great compliment of handing us our dignity and waiting in courtly deference for us to want an honest, free relationship with Him.

This is too good to be untrue! He respects our doubts, welcomes our questions, knows both sides of us well, even the side that isn't able to love.

I have told Him often how tough I think He made this old world. I ask Him recurrently,

"Where are You in this anguish?"

Immediately and always He is real, and He changes my despair. I get whittled down to my right size, all right, but charged with a shot of joy. Still my trudging self, in part, I get a new sense of gentle momentum and present motive.

Well, after some vivid instances of giving the Lord and each other a piece of our minds, no holds barred, your father and I knew that God really does hold the universe together, and is far bigger than our threats, thrashings, questions. We knew that He welcomes the honest, the bold, the vital. It's the Milquetoasts who weary Him.

In Matthew it says the unfaithful servant shall

be cut in two. Is this a slashing way of saying that it is eternally unbearable to remain in undeclared compartments?

It is hellish to have great cannonballs of self-hatred within us. It is hellish to be separated from our real selves.

But if both compartments, both sides of ourselves, are on speaking terms with each other and with the Creator, haven't we begun the Eternal trek here and now?

Instead of dragging our hostilities behind us, we had, by the time Wayne was sick, delivered enough bombs to each other and to God to have started the Eternal trek without fear of cut-apartness, that instinctive dread of death.

But this only dawned on me lately, delayed learner that I am.

13.

The other evening a supper guest said in capsulized simplicity,

"All day I am doing nothing."

Her laziness had become redemptive loafing and she was wearily grateful.

Today I am doing nothing, weary to the bone and no bounce within.

Nothing, that is, but talk to the painter, catch up on last week's papers, comfort my grandchild, and weep over a dying identity and study for a new one.

While I am doing nothing up in the sunny backyard, barefooted in the chaise, the welcome sky above our beloved trees, I am looking at the translation of a song I've sung for many years, the better to sing it again on the morrow. The words jump out at me from Brahms's "Feldeinsamkeit"—loneliness in an open meadow.

The German words have it,

"It is as though I have been dead a long time and am blessedly drifting in eternal realms with those clouds that I see from this solitary summer field."

Because "dead" has always meant to me not "lifeless" but "more alive in extra dimensions," the lines have sung themselves into me,

"For a long time I have sensed a joyful drum whose glory-roll is heightened as I rest my eyes and my soul on the beauty of those far-distant, lit-up clouds, from my happy solitude in this sunny spot."

All these thirty years I have sung it that way, seeing the great skies above my South Dakota horizons and my childhood's backyard. But today the translation gave me a fresh charge.

"It is as though I long ago had died."

Long ago I was more alive than now! It reminded me of Wordsworth's "Ode on Intimations of Immortality."

> Not in entire forgetfulness,
> And not in utter nakedness,
> But trailing clouds of glory do we come
> From God, who is our home.

We come from and return to a glory life, our days now the interim reverberation!

When I was fourteen, a sixty-year-old Welsh

scholar, musician, and homiletics professor, David Jones Evans, wrote into my old-fashioned autograph book the opening lines of that great ode:

> There was a time when meadow, grove and
>   stream,
> The earth, and every common sight,
>   To me did seem
>   Appareled in celestial light,
> The glory and the freshness of a dream.

The lines came through to me then as "the glory and the freshness of celestial light." I loved the light of our great horizons of prairie, mountain and field. *Celestial* light I therefore knew intuitively.

My lonely lassitude on the chaise was suddenly set in the larger context of Heaven here and now. The bounce returned to my do-nothing bones because I saw vividly one more reason why I had had no fear of death.

I ouched my way barefoot from the upper level of the backyard, in order to get paper and pencil. To the painter I said,

"You know about 'easy does it'?" He is a real AA. I'm an alcoholic without the bottle.

"I am doing *nothing* up there in the backyard, and I get another chapter for the little book I think I'm writing."

He knew just what I meant.

To do nothing, to dream, to have an inner emptiness that becomes an inner knowingness, to think long thoughts, to rest on a soundless certitude of a celestial strength and glory that is "fore, aft, and within"—

I had been doing that off and on for thirty-some years!

Wayne knew those lines of Wordsworth's as well as I did, but he had reveled in the *theories* of eternal verities. By September their actualities were apparently stirring in him. How else could he have said, over that high breakfast bar,

"You're an outpost of the Kingdom"?

O joy! And what a switch! For years he had had reservations about my individualistic, experiential interpretation and articulation of everything. Now my intractable spiritual bounce and passion were a lifeline to him. For years a kooky mystic, now I was a lighthouse.

My heart bowed in grateful joy but I didn't say a word. He was glimpsing with soundless certitude the celestial glory from which we came and to which he probably would be returning sooner than I.

14.

Warmed as he was at our hearthside that fall, sitting in his Irish green jacket, lifted by great music, inspired by great books, ministered to by you buoyant dear ones, his warmth of "inward knowingness" showed itself in several ways.

In one sermon he said that the "why?" of tragedy, grief and pain is a self-regarding question that we are not equipped to answer, one which can lead to bitterness and despair. Not "why?" but "to what end?" No matter how broken or shattered our life might be, there is always some work that we alone can do, someone who needs what only we can give. With trouble comes the priceless gift of understanding others' distress. With profound trouble comes a deep closeness with others, an end in itself.

In another sermon at the end of September, planned for all the Sunday school children, two-thirds of them black, he sang a current favorite civil rights song in the pulpit: " 'How many roads..., how many seas..., how many times . . . , 'til men feel close as brothers? . . . The answer is blowin' in the wind.' "

He knew the youngsters heard a good bit in their song, and to all of us, astounded at his singing, he said,

"All the wonder and mystery of God's direct and indirect affirmation of His Creation are in those lines 'The answer is blowin' in the wind.'

"All the mighty potential for new steps toward justice, brotherhood and peace are hidden in you. Be alert, be faithful, and pray that Christ will use your life creatively through His Church to answer some great need in the world before you die. Amen."

I heard also the premonition of the personal answer coming in those lines, for he had said at the beginning,

"This is the grand full Trinity season of the year when we give full rein to the Holy Spirit, the Personal Loving Force of God that blows like a mighty wind across the face of the world.

"You have been a living channel of that Spirit to me. Without that Spirit blowing through your prayers, I would not be here."

The following week he sent these words to those who continued to send messages daily:

Dear Friend,

Another and somewhat more painful chapter has been written in our experience during these recent weeks. Steady aches in hip and spine and leg, together with some other disturbing developments, such as a slowing down of my ability to swallow, have brought on some hours of misery by day and by night.

"Pills and capsules that once were efficacious have diminished in their power to relieve. I am getting X-rays daily now, beamed toward lymph glands in neck and chest. Radiation skin burns in armpits get sorer as the series nears completion. Heavy dosage of X-rays in my hip, started this week, have mercifully relieved a sharp ache there.

The way has been steep, the road rough and dark with fears. At times, to have one more thing go wrong was almost more than we could bear. I say "we" because Margaret shares deeply this load of trouble.

One of our church members who has been remodeling his basement said it looked like "a disaster area." That's the way my body looks and feels.

But the miracle is that I am here at all. And one gradually learns to live with pain. When you take pain pills and the pain mounts for awhile before diminishing, this is almost worse than bearing it without the pills or capsules. The experience of bearing pain without help becomes one of cleansing and purification, at times.

I didn't get to our service of prayers for healing last evening, but I learned from a friend that some sixty people were there. I have been able to test more closely the effects of intercession. I noticed during the wakeful hours of this past night a great sense of peace and calm coming down over me.

There is a real strengthening of the spirit that comes as a result of being prayed for. This enables one to handle the problem far more easily, to get above it, to see it diminish. I have learned a new respect for the body in all this.

We live in hope that a day will arrive when these troubles will be overcome in victory. The steady support of my dear wife (whom I jokingly call "sweet bird of my old age") and family, the loving concern of the church people at Augustana as well as that of a wide circle of friends in distant places, has been a priceless boon, for which I thank God day and night. Too, I have found the doctors I have met to be sensitive, dedicated, and able to convey a deep sense of the affirmative of life.

I have drawn close to Job and have a new appreciation for Habakkuk, who wrote,

"Though the fig tree do not blossom, nor fruit be on the vines, the produce of the olive fail and the fields yield no food, the flock be cut off from the fold and there be no herd in the stalls, yet will I rejoice in the Lord, I will joy in the God of my salvation." Nor should I forget to mention the peculiar comfort which I find in the memory of Jesus hanging on a cross for me.

And from there it is not far to—New Life! With my heart full of gratitude to you . . .

Wayne R. Woods and family

15.

When his lungs became involved, in late October, he went into the hospital for a week and wrote from there:

> Since October 3rd there has been a major turn for the better and yet another set-back in a case of pneumonia in my right lung. The cancer and the 92 X-rays I have sustained have played havoc with my strength and resistance.
>
> I am taking antibiotic capsules and "fomentations," as the Seventh Day Adventists call them. The latter are heavy woolen compresses soaked in boiling water, wrung out by machine and applied with towel protection for the skin to chest and back for 30 minutes, with a fresh hot compress every ten minutes.

Your head meanwhile is wrapped in a towel soaked in ice water. And your feet are lifted and put into hot water, as hot as you can stand it. This is a powerful remedy for what ails you, but it is also enervating. I seem very weak. I am getting naps in morning and afternoon. The pneumonia makes me sweat in bed, day and night. So there you have it. I feel pretty "wrung out."

The X-rays have been discontinued. The cancer has been arrested (conquered?) in abdomen, shoulder, upper chest (we hope); but an annoying ache remains in the hip and spine, with a reference pain to the left leg, where some ten inches of shin-skin is partially numb. This problem is fairly well controlled by Darvon capsules.

I am so grateful to have been able to preach and help at Augustana until mid-October. At that time the doctor called for a two-month rest to rebuild my strength. The Church Council has graciously granted me a two-month leave of absence. How I long to be well again!

Because my condition continues to be both precarious and painful, a new decision has been made. With my wife's and my doctor's approval, I am offering myself to the National Institutes of Health here in Bethesda. A recent bulletin indicates they are doing cancer research with lymphosarcoma. Negotiations are being made through my doctor to see if I can be admitted. This will be an exciting new venture, for which I shall need the further benefit of your prayers. I hope I can stand up to it.*

God is a steadfast help. He sustains us and lights the path for each new step. I have put my heart's trust in Him, come what may. Thanks loads for your love, your faith, your friendship.

Wayne

That month he signed his body over for research purposes to the George Washington University Medical School. He wanted it to be of some use in the medical field! He asked his associate to help prepare him for death and several times they sequestered themselves in the den. He took communion with its confession and absolution and they talked about his hopes for life even while looking toward very possible death. He wrote down some last notes to his family and asked that a preacher-politician friend in Pittsburgh speak at the memorial service.

An unknown friend sent Louise the money to fly home for a brief visit in October. On one of those warm fall noon-days, she and your dad and I took our hymnals to the park. For twenty minutes we sat on a bench in the golden warmth

*They would not take a case for chemical treatment which had already had the X-ray approach.

and sang very gently in three-part harmony some hymns which Louise already knew the tunes of, for she was reading a Braille hymnal, and no music is given in them. All our notes were accurate, warm, grateful. Each combination of voices is a new instrument, I think, and she and I have that combination in clear memory. We recall only Grieg's hymn from that day, though, as golden as the sunshine and the leaves around us.

Let myriad voices hail his might,
And praise the Lord, who by his word
Hath stablished you in light.

16.

Through the years we had done our own painting and fixing. Your father was very patient with me when it came to getting the right shade of paint for a given area. As we mixed and stirred and slurped from bucket to bucket, and calculated amounts, tubes of color, shadows, and the drying effect, he stood beside me deferent, silent, expectant. When the right shade emerged, a miracle before our eyes, I tried to explain to him my restless dissatisfaction with anything less than that right shade, which I could never have predicted.

"I feel that if you'll just stick by me, the right color will come," I said apologetically.

Said he instantly,

"That's just the way I feel about my sermons. If you will just stay by me while I struggle along, they'll come."

This clear moment didn't return to memory until recently when I asked a friend if she had helped her husband with the remarkable sermon we had just heard ("Psychotherapy and the Soul," no less).

"No, I just sat by him," she told me. "I was just present to him."

Being present to the other person is the kind of support needed for him to find his own thoughts, colors, path. We need not try to find a solution for him, only be present to him, physically, mentally, spiritually.

No one can give another person his path to death, and during those months it didn't occur to me to give your dad any largesse of advice, sympathy, condolence or pity. I was present to him, numbly, deferently and not always kindly.

In my usual November scurry to get tulip bulbs in, I asked him to be present to me, put on hat and coat, sit in a lawn chair, and check from a supervisory distance just how I would place them in a triangular pattern on an astigmatic slope. Red ones and yellow ones went in.

I was in a familiar rotten mood, an old Achilles heel, and as I raked and dug and thumped I said,

"How would *you* like it if you were going to live alone the rest of your life?"

Said he in a dry tone,

"I'd wait a year and then I'd get married again."

"Thanks a lot," I snapped, thinking how

crassly he could transfer tenderness and replace precious me. Then I realized I *should* thank him. He was saying that one relationship had been good enough, thank you, he'd try another.

Well, he was present to me as I crabbed myself out of my mood, and I was present to him as he wrestled with life and death in the cells of body and brain. Neither of us had solutions for the other's pains, but we were each finding our way. I think that if I had flooded him with concern, attention, fussiness, he would have washed up in a heap.

As to those tulips. They have an extra quality of light in them. They are most bright, just the right shade and in the right spot, since there is no grave in any cemetery.

17.

In the latter part of November your dad wrote his last letter, one that expressed so well the changes he was aware of.

Dear Partner on the Way,

You may believe it or not, but I am convinced that a miracle is taking place in me. And the only way I can account for it is that Christ is working this great change *through your love and your prayers.*

In the very face of a number of worsening conditions since latter October—for the most part a lack of appetite, and therefore daily battles to eat a little several times, often being unable to keep it down; a steady loss of weight with a frightening waste of the body (I now weigh around 125 pounds); a slow drain of physical strength making walking uncertain at times; the loss of the use of my right eye; swelling ankles; pneumonia in the right lung; repeated sweats at night requiring thorough changes—in the very teeth of all this a wonderful miracle is happening. Let me explain.

I can laugh at the whole business. An incredible humor bubbles up through it constantly. I find my heart running over with the Master's "good cheer" (facing death on the morrow, He said, "In the world you have tribulation; but be of good cheer . . ."). It is as if inward fetters of mind and spirit have been struck from me and I am gloriously free to live. I am full of a boundless gratitude. I have the world's most wonderful woman as my help-meet. I have never been so sensitive to discern love and to give it. I have never been able to use my emotions as fully as I can now. I can almost feel the very pulse of God. Our home is simply flooded with an unearthly beauty, continually being generated by the Holy Spirit. The joyous Christ is here, sitting with me by day and by night. And the Omnipotent God reigns in indescribable majesty and power with the whole of creation and all of human history like two straws in His mighty hand.

All this is the golden harvest of your faithful caring and praying!

So—to each one of you I send a dripping dipperful of thanks and joy and love.

Wayne

P.S. Praise God with me! The pneumonia is gone. Under X-rays (I've had 114 so far) my lung is clearing and my right eye improves daily. The night sweats are diminishing. Swollen ankles are near normal size. Darvon capsules every two hours keep the pain in hip and leg undercover. I am still able to go outside for a walk (on Margaret's arm), to travel in the car once in awhile to church, movie, concert, and even on an occasional visit. I can still read and think and pray. Each day is a gift, a feast, a banquet. Glory, Hallelujah!

18.

On a Tuesday in late November I drove Wayne to an all-day meeting of Lutheran ministers. It was only five minutes from our home, and he felt he could return at noon for his simple meal and some rest, and then go back if he found the strength to do so.

In these meetings the brethren were beginning to offer each other an honest, therapeutic, supportive exchange. I listened in on this one and enjoyed it immensely. Wayne found to his great joy that the unaffected comments he made, coming from the depths of the personal battle he was fighting and that every man must fight if he chooses life in the broadest terms, were of value to his friends. This lifted his own spirits greatly and made him want to preach on the following Sunday.

Both services were conducted by his associate, and until time for each sermon Wayne was in his study stretched out on the long couch. We saw him limp into the chancel on the arm of an acolyte, very thin, one eyelid drooping. He sat in a wing chair with a pillow supporting his back, at a high round table that held microphone and manuscript. His gratitude, joy and effort were unforgettable to all of us.

On the following Friday our David, Mary Carol's husband, drove him up to the hospital for his treatment. When the X-ray man wanted him to stay, right then and there, in order to build up his strength with intravenous feedings, he stubbornly said he had another sermon to preach. I went up, to try and help with the logic, and then phoned our own doctor, who said, "Sure, he can preach." Only then did Wayne let himself be aided into the familiar wheelchair and be propelled upstairs, loud flannel jacket, red hunter's cap and all.

Early Sunday morning December first, I took his clerical togs up to his room, waited while he slowly dressed, helped him into the wheelchair, and pushed him down and out to the car. As on the previous Sunday two acolytes helped him with his robes and he lay on the couch in the study until just time for the sermon in each service. He was visibly weaker.

Immediately after the sermon the acolytes helped him out of his robes and into his heavy winter coat and hat. We went out the rear door, into the car, and back to the hospital.

I don't think he said a word on the journey back. I felt the silence, because ordinarily the Sunday services gave him bounce and verve, reactions and plans. I parked the car, left him in it while I brought the wheelchair out, placed it, opened the car door, held the door and the chair while he slowly got himself from one seat to the other. And there were still no words.

The X-ray man had seriously objected to the venture, knowing the strength it would use up. Our own doctor's theory had been much like my own—let him pace himself in the occupations that were fruitful ones for him. And now he seemed almost ready to slip away as he lay back in his bed.

But even as we had freed him to pace himself along his path, so he, perceiving a path I had been pacing myself in, now gave me great freedom in it. I had typed his last two sermons and with some impudence had changed small parts of them. As he lay back on his bed he extended his raised arm toward me feebly and said with slight motions of the Cross,

"I ordain you a minister . . .

". . . waive seminary . . .

". . . Father, Son, . . . Holy Ghost."

The moment held humor for both of us. With the unadorned prerogative of the very brave he confirmed an identity I had sensed for several years. It was the lieutenant colonel saying that any foot soldier fired up with the general's purposes carries equivalent insignia.

I think now that we each communicated to the other an identity that strengthened and released. We freed each other to be, in thrilling ways.

That night was a frightening one for him, and the next morning he wanted to "call off the intravenous feedings and go downhill fast." I dissuaded him, saying that we take as good care of the dying as we can, giving them the comforts of cleanliness, liquids in the system, and so on. Thereafter he accepted the ministrations and treatments of the next month with grace and courage, even though each involved some fortitude on his part.

19.

Months after Wayne died, you told me, Mary Carol, that his face always lit up when I came into his hospital room. I hadn't realized that I was "playing from strength" and thereby strengthening.

Many people seem to think they should leave their own vigorous selves outside the door and in the presence of tragedy put on a tragic veil and a commiserating mien. They do it with blind people and misshapen cripples as well as the dying. Are they imagining there is no strength in the tragic and no frailty in health? Each diamond has many sides, and the side that flashes strength will pick up and enlarge the bright facets from the other side.

Pills, naps, treatments, sweats and drying-outs brought no crumpling solicitude from me. I can recall only one occasion when I was the zealous caretaker. Although it was a good thing at that moment, it nearly crumpled *me*.

In the latter part of October we went to a symphony concert at Constitution Hall. Your dad was only able to sit through half the program, and when we left the building, a full icy wind was blowing down the empty street. I love the wind, but as we leaned into it, I saw his faltering steps and immediately started calculating his strength against the distance to the parking lot. Looking frantically around for a taxi, my eye caught sight of a car with a light on it. I waved it down, talked the cruising patrolmen out of their rules, and collapsed silently in the back corner after we were both in. My overreaction undid me! What if I had always been supercharged with protective concern? Would we not both have been seriously weakened?

When our Pittsburgh friends came for Thanksgiving, their shock at your dad's emaciated frame must have come through in spite of their natural cheerfulness, and he felt it. As he and I drove back to the house on Friday morning, after seeing a nerve specialist about that dead space on his leg, he didn't get out of the car immediately but said in a quarrelsome tone,

"Does everybody have me for dying?"

"Well," said I, groping for some partial truth, "medically speaking, you are."

"So are you," he snapped, flinging at me the well-known fact of degeneration in everyman's cells.

We got out of the car. The agonizing shock on the faces of long-absent friends had brought out in him not joy in the life still left but anger. They didn't share his hopeful battle and didn't predicate victory on the basis of the fight.

In life and in death, relationships are strengthened if we bring our best selves to them. Too many people bring pity, which is often a cloak for profound aversion, consternation or rejection. Compassion clarifies but pity weakens, and relationships are quickly unhinged. Some folks evidenced such profound dismay, they seemed to want strength from Wayne, rather than to convey it to him.

Almost three weeks before your dad died, the doctor told me he had only a few days to go. When I came back into the room Wayne asked me what the conversation in the hall had been about. Here was the agreed-on honesty again, hard but healthy.

"He says you only have a few days to go."

He looked like a small boy shocked to the core.

"You've known it all along," I said gently.

We decided to ask family members from a distance to come for a day or two while he was still able to communicate with them, for the weird "hallucies" had begun, when he repeated meaningless syllables endlessly. The overwhelming emotion in the face of one of them was very hard on him.

"I am almost undone," he said after they left.

At home later to the rest of us she regretfully reviewed her lack of control, for she knew better than to weep in his presence. I have thought since that perhaps I was enabled during those months to carry few debilitating emotions when around him because he had done likewise for me in other kinds of exigencies!

20.

From here to the hospital it's five minutes in the car. The entrance we used was flanked by a fair incline from the parking area. After getting out of the car I had to lug myself up that incline, three times a day at least. Even when I stayed all night the last three weeks, I returned to the house two and three times a day.

To my mind, if a dear one is sick at home you leave him alone to sleep it off, but you're close at hand for whatever he wants of food, conversation, diversion, comfort. If he's in the hospital you're close at hand for whatever seems helpful. You stay cheerfully present, available, quiet. You provide a buoyancy that says without words:

"This isn't the end, dear one.

"There's lots going, parallel to us and ahead of us."

But one Saturday evening I had no bounce, no desire to go up to that room whatever. As I trudged up the incline from the car in the December night I had to say,

"Lord, You be in this."

What happened was thrilling. I don't know who suggested it, but we decided to role-play. He would be John the Baptist and I would be Wayne R. Woods, before Jesus started to preach. We found ourselves making up conversation about locusts and Essene literature and communal life. We were solicitous about the Frail Cripple in our midst, the Suffering Servant prophesied by Isaiah. He would need a strong-armed, bellowing preacher to prepare the way ahead of him if He decided to start out in the villages with His message. For to those of us who had lived a monastic life with Him for several years, His insights and leadership had become crucial.

Here was the gal who had often wished she were a man! For half an hour she lived in one man's mind, responded to the real and imaginary levels in another man's mind, while they fancied themselves in a most thrilling juncture of history when several men were aware of the More than themselves in their midst.

What joy! We found ourselves with insights we knew to be of recurrent human dimensions, capable at depth and height of seeing what men have always seen and felt at depth and height! I have never known a richer half-hour.

The following week we decided to beguile an evening's time again with role-playing. He was sitting in the big chair, his head propped on his arm, a little red pillow helping his back. I was curled on his wound-up bed, tired and peevish. We were both just weary enough to not care much *what* we said. He would be Luther and I would be Katherine, before they were married!

I can't say I know nothing about Luther's mind, because I got resumes of all Wayne's reading through the years. And where other couples discuss fishing equipment versus skiing equipment, we crossfired on the creative existential elements, positive and negative, in Luther, Kierkegaard, Bonhoeffer, Lincoln, Jefferson, Gandhi, Michaelangelo, whomever he was reading at the time. I'm a contingent thinker, much to my dismay now, and your dad was half my education for twenty-five years. He could be shaving and I could be in the tub, and it would be *Luther* we'd be talking about. But I don't expect anybody to believe that.

What I know about Katherine could all go under the heading of "tüchtige Hausfrau"—a great provider from kitchen, gardens and flocks.

I essayed some feeble remark about my ducks and orchards, trying to keep in mind that he was a scholarly man with many strong minds stimulating and supporting him. We parried a bit and he broached the subject of marriage in general. For all my great enjoyment of many men's minds through the years, as Katherine I couldn't cope with the prospect of being a supportive ingredient to a masculine theological world! And I thought Martin was speaking historically when he said,

"Wouldn't you like to marry my friend?"

Katherine was sunk in petulance, with no energy to help the monks become balanced pastors with families.

"No."

Was this a "speak for yourself, John," moment?

Now I'm all for marriage, for valued relationship, but here I was refusing it when he came back to it again.

"Wouldn't you want to marry my friend?"

"No."

"Why not?"

"Because I don't think men want tenderness."

What a revelation! From nine levels down I was acknowledging weariness at meeting men's minds, and would they please meet my deep need for gentleness—I who was afraid to be very gentle myself!

There followed one of the happiest weeks of our lives, when he was able to hold the full cup of tenderness, before he sank into the long stretches of evident brain-ravage.

"How much has to be taken away," he said, "before you find the real thing."

21.

All this time your father had been in bed only when in the hospital, and even then he was up and out many times a day. At home when he napped he simply put on his long woolen robe and stretched out in Steve's room.

He respected personal discipline of all kinds. He had retained his high school interest in long-distance running, and when an important Fourth of July race was held in our own Pittsburgh streets, do you remember how we all hopped in and out of the car at every spot the runners would pass? After the race Wayne queried the winner as to his training. He had run twelve and thirteen miles every day for six years and was aiming for the Olympics. Steady does it!

A month before Wayne was operated on, we were at Gettysburg on the hill behind the Seminary Chapel. Everybody was taking a breather after some thrilling lectures. The slope down to a great tree was enticing, my legs were aching for a run, and I said,

"Race you to the tree!"

He paused a long time before he took me up on it. He knew of the lump, and had felt increasing fatigue, but had not yet told anyone. Of course he won, but the length of that pause comes back to me now as the soul's instant debate: "I'm not able, I am able." The habits of years took him fleetly down the hill, with three growths in his body right then.

When we painted the trim on our creosote shingle bungalow in the summer of '62, he was the one who stayed with it hour after hour, day after day, carefully scraping and mending first, putting up wire against the pigeons under the overhang, and conquering his fears on the extension ladder. All this on vacation, the weeks when Steve glowed with the joy of making a doghouse with his dad's help.

When he became ill, he knew from experience, habit and reading that all gains are costly, whether in sickness or health, war or peace, storm or calm, requiring vision and endurance. His heroes were Gandhi, Lincoln, Schweitzer, Kagawa, Comparing his tribulations with theirs, he seemed to feel he had no right to complain. He had been immersed most of his life in lines such as these from Catton's *A Stillness at Appomattox,* which he had used in a sermon that fall:

"How often," wrote one soldier, "the words 'cruel war' are uttered, and how glibly people beyond the reach of its influence talk of misery caused by it . . . but not one-thousandth of the real misery is even guessed at by those who are not eye-witnesses to its horrors."

He endured the battering effects of 130 X-ray treatments on six major areas of his body without ever complaining. In September when he was still driving the car and an ache had turned up in a new spot, he leaned out the window before driving away and said,

"Sometimes I'm about ready to throw in the sponge."

This was as much as he ever said. He got wittier and funnier as he got frailer, and he was a joy to be with.

As he grew weaker he deliberately stirred up the life forces within him by getting up when he felt bad, and taking a walk when he felt worse. A friend long versed in cancer nursing told me privately that a close friend in the same profession who had contracted a malignancy in the lymph system had closed up her business affairs and lain down and died in a month, not wanting to prolong what she knew the course would be. My friend also said,

"Wayne will have longer to live because he's working at it so hard."

I can still see the weary frame that kept on

walking, holding onto side or hip or onto my arm. Even in November I drove him to several meetings which he had helped plan and to which he had a contribution to make. Martin Luther King was to speak at one of them, but had to send an associate at the last minute. Wayne's countenance was a blanched gray-green, but he was there. To all of us it was stark courage. He had a right to preach on discipline that fall. "As your days are, so shall your strength be."

When he went into the hospital after Thanksgiving, it was with the hope that the X-rays, the food, the intravenous feedings might catch up with the enemy and reverse the direction of weight loss. He clung to every small item, even when the effort for each seemed to be wearing him out more than helping him.

You know how those nurses' aides come in brightly saying,

"And will you have some breakfast this morning?"

By the middle of December he had kept down little more than water for days, but he slowly sat up and said obediently in a hopeful voice that broke my heart,

"I'll try."

For a while they weighed him every morning, looking for ounces. When it had taken two of us to get his tottering frame onto the scales at the side of the bed, several mornings in a row, I privately burst a gusset to the doctor and said, "What's all this for?"

A similar reaction to the X-rays finally brought an end to them. He had been going down to the therapy department in a wheel-chair, hardly able to sit up. I had serious silent resentment toward those endless debilitating treatments until I found out after he died that they had undoubtedly decreased his pain, which no amount of morphia can cover up in some cases. Then I was grateful, and ashamed of my private recalcitrance, for he had needed blessed little medication.

Each morning I read aloud to him the greetings that came in the mail. With one card came a little tract entitled "A Chapel in the Soul." I read the words of Brother Lawrence:

"It is not necessary for being with God to be always at church; we make an oratory of our heart wherein to retire from time to time, to converse with Him in meekness, humility and love. An oratory of our heart. That is, a chapel in the soul."

These were the words to reach a man who loved the altar, the liturgy, the lessons for the church year, the man whose own voice had lifted many a heart with its beauty and sincerity. The Source of all newness and all strength always gets through in words and concepts that are clear to *us*. Flat on his back, Wayne could literally turn his heart into a well-loved chapel and in a labor of heart and mind and soul find some peace for body and mind.

When I came back in the afternoon I knew he had found a new domain, knit a new stitch, for he said,

"I've been making an oratory of my heart. It helps."

As the weird "hallucies" continued, he said he had a terrible time organizing his mind, and he described his condition as "endless misery." I was the last one to recognize the brain damage that others had expected, for there were clear moments every day right up to the end.

With most of his conscious mind most of the time he thought he could win the big battle going on in his lymph system. Three nights before he died, when the battered brain needed help in reviewing the case, he asked,

"Why am I not making it?"

I had to remind him that the surgeon had given him a maximum of three months, that without the X-ray treatments he probably wouldn't have lasted one month, that it had gotten a big head start long before we knew about it, and that we had had seven months instead of one. When he realized that the silent head start had given the enemy the advantage, and not any lack of fight on his part, he seemed satisfied.

A couple of nights before he died, when he was

fairly clear, very weary, and unable to stop fighting, he spoke as though to himself and to me and to God.

"How do you do it? Do you just let down?"

"You just trust Jesus," I said. "You trust the everlasting arms."

22.

I need to sit and assimilate, frequently. The Quakers call it centering down. Some call it meditation. I call it my quiet time.

On the second day of January, the afternoon, the sunshine, the patient and the bedclothes all had a fresh, washed look. I had been afraid he might choke to death in an agonizing struggle with phlegm or breath. I was at the end of my tether as far as staying at night any more, and I could be of no more help because he was unconscious so much of the time. He had sat up beside me the evening before, our arms around each other in frailty and support, in his usual heroic effort to effect some change within. At noon Louise and I both discerned his muffled, thick, gallant "Good-bye" after she leaned over him and wordlessly shook his hand in farewell, for back to school she must go. She had been with us when we valued her help the most.

As I sat at the side of his bed for an hour in the afternoon sunshine, his throat seemed to settle, his mouth broadened as though to make his leather dry lips form a smile, and after five minutes of much slower breathing, another breath just didn't come. I cried with joy and relief and gratitude because I had wanted to be there at the end.

I could have sat there peaceably another hour, but the afternoon shift of nurses changed and one bobbed in and bobbed out again speedily. Silently and speedily she returned with a more important nurse carrying a stethoscope. They both padded out and returned with an intern. All this to validate death?

Meanwhile I'm sitting there in great peace. Why can't they leave me alone? Why do they have to rush all this?

The intern asked me to leave the room. I stood outside a few seconds and marched right back in again, furious.

"Listen, I've been here all along. I don't think I should have to go out of the room now. What do you have to do that's so important, close his eyes or something?" Wayne looked nightmarish, his ninety pounds providing no flesh around his eye-sockets.

I've forgotten what the intern said. He didn't perceive that I was happy and grateful, and that I had been interrupted.

I cupped my hand around the beautiful bone structure of Wayne's cheek and chin, now horribly hollow and said,

"You've been a great fighter, dear one."

There were only the red pillow and the green jacket to take home. The intern offered a tranquilizer.

"Good grief, what for?"

Did I want someone to drive me home?

"Mercy, no. It's only five minutes from here."

As I got out of the car at home Louise came out onto the porch.

"Daddy died," I said with peculiar happiness. It was great tidings to bear.

"I'm so glad," said she.

We all cried together and cried some more.

Weeks later, I asked a friend,

"Why can't they let people *be,* in *peace?*"

"Because there's no peace in *them,*" came the instant answer.

What was interrupted then has been assimilated since, in more than one quiet time.

23.

All fall Wayne had listened to great music, including Rachmaninoff's Second Piano Concerto. Once he said musingly,

"You could play this at my service."

His real instructions came after that last sermon when he went straight back to the hospital bed. When he suggested withdrawing the intravenous feedings and going downhill fast, he added,

"You can sing some of the hymns we've loved."

This was a poignant directive. We had acquired separate enthusiasms in the hymnal, but what we loved was inevitably contagious to the other.

I chose hymns, Scripture and prayers that would stir the living rather than bemoan the dead. It was a thrilling memorial service. There were just two gleaming vases of red carnations on the altar. I had thought about putting your dad's Ben Franklin reading glasses up there, just to see if anybody would notice them. They were a recent hilarious addition, allowing room for his copious eyebrows. But I forgot.

When a startled churchman obediently read aloud my choices from Ephesians and Romans, my heart sank.

"Do they really understand my hopes?"

I wanted the experience to be illuminating, not one that would let the heaviness in our spirits continue. But who would guess that?

"According to the riches of his glory he may grant you to be strengthened with might through his Spirit in the inner man, and that Christ may dwell in your hearts through faith; that you, being rooted and grounded in love, may have power to comprehend with all the saints what is the breadth and length and height and depth, and to know the love of Christ which surpasses knowledge, that you may be filled with all the fullness of God."

A familiar repentant feeling humbled my hopes and I said, as though to Wayne,

"I've pulled another boner. This is too odd."

I had the feeling that he upheld my creative venture, shored me up again and said,

"It's okay, kid."

So there were no traditional funeral verses. I hoped that all the frail mortals who are part of the Church, and the many at funerals who are far from it, would equally be uplifted by a joyful expression of the Creator's presence and power. There we sat singing with all our loved ones,

> O how shall I receive Thee,
> How greet Thee, Lord, aright?
> All nations long to see Thee,
> My Hope, my heart's delight!

One of us *was* seeing Him in a new way.

And for this small sinner to sing with hundreds of others,

> There's a wideness in God's mercy,
> Like the wideness of the sea;
> There's a kindness in His justice,
> Which is more than liberty.
>
> There is no place where earth's sorrows
> Are more felt than up in heaven;
> There is no place where earth's failings
> Have such kindly judgment given.
>
> For the love of God is broader
> Than the measures of man's mind,
> And the heart of the Eternal
> Is most wonderfully kind.

I had the distinct feeling that those cosmopolitan Washingtonians, country lambs at heart, were grateful for the old-fashioned balm. I myself had needed it for many years and needed it again now.

It was plain fun to have steered the great group into singing the rolling Welsh tune, "Guide me, O thou great Jehovah."

And we *sang*. With the choir in the rear balcony and the singing preachers in the chancel, we soared.

Later in the service a quartet sent out over our heads the lovely strains the three of us had sung in the park in October,

> Behold a host like mountains bright!
> Lo! who are these arrayed in white,
> A glorious band, with palms in hand
> Around the throne of Light?
> Lo, these are they who overcame
> Great tribulation in his name,
> And with his blood the Lamb of God
> Hath washed away their shame.
> Before God's face they sing and pray,
> Their voices blend with angels' lay,
> And all conspire, a joyous choir,
> To laud him night and day.

We all were the heavenly choir singing before God's face, and I think a good many of us knew it.

Afterward we broke bread together with a little coffee and had a hearty handshake all around. It did us good to greet each other in festive love and gratitude rather than in somber woe.

There was no concerto as background music for this happy service. I think I know now why Wayne first thought of it. Filtering through every cadence come sustaining hope, gentle exultation and renewal. But by our singing rather than our listening we ourselves were renewed, as he had been.

How could there be a grave?

Epilogue

Autumn, 1973

When I needed great trust in the next life, I had it and still have it. Now when I have needed zest for this one, it is being given to me. Since you know several chapters of my spiritual journey, let me tell you the most recent one.

My life in the Church of The Saviour has brought me to a new opening, as John Woolman might say, after some hard and lonely terrain. The years in the orthodox church, some in a congregation as a soloist after Wayne died, never answered a need to hear the insights and vision which Gordon Cosby has. In '69 I returned to the little fellowship, the original destination of our deliberate spiritual embarkation in '56!

All membership here is lived out in small mission groups committed to Christ in the daily disciplines of both an inward journey and an outward one. With "no place else to go" from my basic solitariness, I gradually reached toward real fellowship, never dreaming what was in store for me when I chose to become a corporate person.

My first group let me simply listen and shed my preacher's wife stance. The second group—New Life!—was formed to implement a meld of techniques for confirmation, confrontation and confession, exactly so that our negative feelings aren't swept under a personal rug with the lump obvious to others. At the same time, we actively seek out and confirm each other's strengths, thereby learning what unique gifts might be brought to light and given for strengthening of the Body, in joy and freedom.

With their commitment to Christ and the help of the Holy Spirit, the mission group members pulled the residue of sadness from my bones, confronted me with the feelings I thought were safely walled off, and enabled me to wash them out in the warmth of their support and daily prayers. With my defenses gone, I could accept their love and concern. I now have more than one good mind and heart to think and grow with.

Knowing I had several assorted gifts in my pack, I started looking for the deepest or "best" one. For years, in splendid martyrdom, I had maintained that the vicissitudes of life had prevented me from nurturing or focusing on any but the ones I used to earn a living. What was I feeling "called" to now?

My gifts with visually impaired students had been developed through long experience with my daughter but carried an invisible discomfiture I couldn't locate. After months of hassling the issue with myself, my journal, the Lord and my friends, I could finally say to Him,

"I choose to try to respond to Your influence and directions as distinct from those other powers and principalities at work, and I choose to believe that it is You who has been nudging me these past two years, not some annoying quirks."

I resigned my job to focus on this one gift and to explore the creative arts and freedom in general. For two weeks I felt beautifully virtuous. Then the long haul began.

You never know what the Lord is up to. In order to tie up the package of this manuscript I had to review the twenty-eight-year relationship in the context of the years before and since. New insights surfaced day after day, exactly the ones I needed. I saw clearly that my problems after Wayne's death were not caused by widowhood or by life in a parsonage but by a basic dislocation of my deepest self. Since early childhood I had tuned out my own real feelings and had become a support to someone else's. I had become an auxiliary, contingent person, a support for others' needs and dreams. My sense of valid personhood was an undeveloped territory. My values, goals and decisions had not been generated out of a conscious free center. I am mortified to say that I felt and thought and acted largely through other people's needs and goals. I should live so long and learn so late?

When I tried to will the will of God in the use of my talents, I received the great gift of my own self. So this is what the Lord had in mind for these arduous months! I took a baby's step when I thought I was taking an elephant's, and moved into deeper terrain within myself. Praise be!

The carefully hidden bitterness over my portion has really turned to gratitude for all of its ingredients. I want to say loudly that the miracle was not wrought by professional or academic zeal, nor by familial commitments, nor even by my own well-established quiet times. It was done by choosing to become a corporate person in Christ, in a group that wanted to heal others as well as themselves.

Peace having been made with myself and my brethren, my hostilities and envy are going out the door. May I humbly and freely choose to live from my real center, in His munificent provision, using each gift as He so nudges.